Perfectly Imperfect

How Walking 60 Miles in 3 Days Shed Plenty of Biases

Cathy Miller

Old Lady Biz Publishing

Copyright © 2025 by Cathy Miller

All rights reserved.

ISBN - Paperback: 979-8-9933529-0-9

ISBN – ePub: 979-8-9933529-1-6

No portion of this book may be reproduced in any form without written permission from the publisher or author, except as permitted by U.S. copyright law.

This publication is designed to provide accurate and authoritative information in regard to the subject matter covered. It is sold with the understanding that neither the author nor the publisher has responsibility for the persistence or accuracy of URLs for external or third-party internet websites referred to in this publication and does not guarantee that any content on such websites is, or will remain, accurate or appropriate.

Book Cover by Bryce Kmetz

Back Cover Kintsugi style pottery by Curtis Kotake

Dedicated to my sister, Terry, who inspires me to be a better person. And to my fellow Pink Tahoe Ladies who walked into my heart.

Contents

INTRODUCTION	1
PART ONE	
WHY 60 MILES?	5
1. First Steps	7
2. Why Keep Going?	15
PART TWO	
BUMPING INTO BIAS	27
3. Self-Inflicted Pain	29
4. Seven Cognitive Biases	35
PART THREE	
A JOURNEY OF THE HEART	53
5. #1 – Accept Myself First	55
6. #2 – Appeciate Unique	65
7. #3 – Change Narrative	75
CONCLUSION: Still Walking	81
NOTES	83

| ABOUT THE AUTHOR | 89 |
| ACKNOWLEDGMENTS | 91 |

INTRODUCTION

How could one of the tiniest body parts cause so much pain? It was Day Two of my third sixty-mile, 3-Day Walk for the Cure. I thought losing a lung while navigating the San Diego "hills" was the worst abuse I could do to my old body. Little did I know to look out for the trip down.

Fearing I may blow out a kneecap on the steep decline, I tentatively took a step, instantly screaming out in pain. My teammates rushed over, thinking I fell. I looked down to see my left walking shoe drenched in blood.

When I removed my shoe, I found the culprit. I had ripped off my baby toenail. All the pavement slapping finally captured its victim. Despite the loss of my little toenail buddy, I completed the full sixty miles, the last two miles in my stocking feet.

What was it about this walk that kept me coming back year after year? It took a lot of steps to begin to understand the why behind it all, although I am still learning more each year. Maybe that's why I cannot walk away.

This journey has taught me a lot about myself, the built-in biases we all have, and how those influence what we feel and do.

I'll share what I've learned. My truth won't be your truth. But hopefully you will see the impact of built-in biases on people like us who want to do better.

PART ONE

WHY 60 MILES?

Old Lady Biz Publishing

PART ONE

WHY 60 MILES?

WHAT POSSESSES A FIFTY-ONE-YEAR-OLD woman to walk sixty miles in three days? One word. Cancer.

Up to that point, cancer was not a prominent player in my family's DNA. You had to go back decades to find a single cancer diagnosis in our family history. That all changed when my sister was diagnosed with breast cancer.

I could not fix this problem. But I had to do something. Why not walk sixty miles in three days? Piece of cake, right?

To understand the draw of this event, let's start at the beginning of my journey, exploring how it captured my heart, and why it is I cannot walk away.

First Steps

IN THE LATE NINETIES, I lived in a beautiful part of southern California known as Channel Islands Harbor. While sitting at a traffic light one weekend, I saw a long stream of people (mostly women) walking down the coast.

"What are you all walking for?" I asked.

"To raise money for breast cancer awareness." One woman told me the walk was Friday through Sunday and a total of sixty miles over the three days.

Wow. Really? These were regular people – in all shapes and sizes. A lot like me. I wasn't sure why this event grabbed me from the start, but it did. At the time, I did not know anyone who had breast cancer. All I knew was I wanted to be a part of this.

Then years went by. Like a nagging aunt, I began hearing ads on the radio about the event urging me to sign up. But as life has a way of doing, my best intentions took a back seat to my day-to-day life.

But that all changed with my sister's diagnosis of breast cancer. Cancer became very personal. My sister's diagnosis was all the push I needed to get up off my couch and on to the streets of San Diego.

A Sister's Tale

The year was 2003. I had moved from Redondo Beach back to my beloved San Diego. I first moved to San Diego in 1977 (I told you I was old) and was excited to be back.

Not long after learning about my sister's breast cancer diagnosis, I began hearing the radio ads for the 3-Day Walk. It felt like a hand reaching through the radio and grabbing me around the heart, scolding me to get off my butt and do this.

I began researching what I needed to do to sign up. I discovered that the event had changed hands from the Avon-sponsored one I witnessed at that stoplight all those years before.

Avon ended its 3-Day event participation in 2002. The Susan G. Komen Breast Cancer Foundation took over as the new sponsor for the 3-Day Walk. In 2003, there were only three cities hosting the 3-Day events: Los Angeles, San Francisco and – drum roll please – San Diego.

Meant to be, right? That was the first of many fate-inspired moments that told me I was right where I needed to be.

FATE-INSPIRED MOMENT #1

Moved back to San Diego – one of only three cities hosting the 3-Day Walk

Another connection was the story behind Susan G. Komen. At its core, it is one sister making a promise to another.

> **The Susan G. Komen Story**
>
> Nancy G. Brinker is the sister of Susan G. Komen (Suzy). They spoke on the phone every day, even after Nancy went away to college.
>
> Nancy received a call from Suzy. Suzy's doctor had discovered a lump in her breast. It was the 1970s; people did not openly discuss breast cancer.
>
> After years of suffering, Suzy died from the disease. Nancy made her dying sister a promise. Nancy would do everything within her power to end the emotional and physical pain of breast cancer. The event proves one person really can make a difference!

My sister had not told us about her diagnosis until after her surgery. When Mom called me, Terry was in the middle of her chemotherapy treatment.

Receiving that call was a punch to the gut. I felt helpless and regretted not being able to be with my sister who lived 2,400 miles away.

Participating in the 3-Day Walk was my silent promise to my sister, Terry. I may not be there physically, but I will always be there spiritually.

And it was the promise I made to myself when I first saw those walkers going down the coast. I needed to get involved. After all, walking sixty miles pales in comparison to chemo.

Lacing Up

I played competitive sports most of my life. But I had never done anything like walking sixty miles in three days. And to do that for the first time at the age of fifty-one sounded even more absurd. At first, my mom and friends questioned my sanity. As someone who hates being told I cannot do something, I was even more determined to try.

I read everything the event put out about preparing for this little stroll. I visited a specialty store for a professional fitting for the shoes I would wear. I purchased socks designed for intensive walking. And I followed the walking training guide the event offered. Or tried to.

After moving back to San Diego, my new employer assigned me to a huge project – helping employers comply with the new privacy law, the Health Insurance Portability & Accountability Act (HIPAA). What that meant was traveling all over the U.S.

From Maui and the Big Island to New York, my frequent flyer miles spun like a Vegas one-armed bandit. While I loved traveling to some of our nation's most beautiful spots, there was one major problem. I just signed up for the sixty-mile, 3-Day Walk. When was I going to train? How was I going to schedule training when work had me traveling to sixteen cities all over the country?

Treadmills, baby. Fortunately, the client was a global chain of luxury hotels. When I was not at home or meeting with the hotel's human resource professionals, you could find me on a treadmill. If you must sweat, why not do it in a luxury hotel's exercise room?

The weekends were my chance to do my heaviest training. Living two blocks from the beach offered stunning training ground. Five-star hotels, ocean-front walks – what can I say, I sacrificed for the Cure.

I continued the weekend walking and treadmill training. I tried to arrange my travel schedule so I would be in town the week of the Walk. One more fantasy shot to hell.

The Monday of the Walk, I was in Boston. On Tuesday, I was in New York and on Wednesday, I was in Washington, D.C. I flew back to San Diego on Thursday, the day before the start of the 3-Day Walk.

What's a little jet lag when walking sixty miles in three days?

Solo Start

As part of my HIPAA project, I worked with Jan, an attorney from an international law firm. When Jan heard about my commitment to the 3-Day, she decided she wanted to participate. Not only was this someone who didn't laugh at my plan, Jan wanted to join me. I was thrilled.

Although our conflicting schedules did not allow us training time together, it was good to know I would have someone take the 3-Day journey with me. Or so I thought.

About a month before the Walk, Jan was traveling for business. She put her briefcase down by her feet and attempted to stow her bigger bag in the overhead compartment. Losing her balance, Jan tripped over her briefcase. Shattered – both Jan's ankle and my dream of a 3-Day partner.

I joked with Jan that if she did not want to do the 3-Day, all she had to do was tell me. She did not need to go to such extremes to get out of it. And just like that, I was on my own.

On the first day of the Walk, I met up with Yvonne who was also walking alone. We quickly bonded as I discovered one of the first truths about the 3-Day. No one walks alone.

We successfully completed Day One (blister-free!) and arranged to meet at a designated spot for Day Two. Day Two arrived but I was unable to locate Yvonne. With 2,000-plus walkers, finding her was like searching for a single snowflake in a blizzard. I was back to flying solo.

Ten miles into Day Two, my feet officially arrived at the 3-Day Walk. Hot spots I snubbed retaliated by morphing into fluid-filled blister bombs, threatening to detonate with every step.

The more I walked, the louder their screeching symphony became. Trying to ignore their discordant tones, I noticed three walkers in front of me who were obviously friends.

Penny was having an animated discussion about her sister-in-law. She mentioned her sister-in-law's full name, and my ears perked up. At least something perked up on my body. Lord knows my feet didn't.

Penny glanced over her shoulder and made eye contact with me.

"Are you walking alone?" she asked.

When I told her I was, Penny invited me to join them. My heart rejoiced at the offer. One thing this lone wolf learned, sharing the 3-Day experience is a lot more fun than going solo.

Penny's friends were Suzanne, a breast cancer survivor, and Suzanne's sister, Diane. I looked at Penny and said, "I didn't mean to eavesdrop, but by any chance, did your sister-in-law work at Prudential in San Francisco?"

Penny blinked in surprise and said, "Yes, she did. Do you know Linda?"

I did know Linda. We worked for the same company for 11 years and I visited Linda's San Francisco office once a month. Is that the Twilight Zone music I hear?

What are the odds that I would happen upon these three walkers at the same time Penny mentioned her sister-in-law by her full name (instead of just Linda)?

Penny, Suzanne, and Diane had walked in the Avon Walks. All three were avid hikers. Yet they accepted my slow, plodding self and my blistered pockets of pain. They lived in the San Francisco Bay area and after walking sixty miles in three days, they hopped on a plane to go back home.

I envied their toned, blister-free bodies but was reenergized as they waved good-bye, yelling, "We'll see you next year!" Although after walking sixty miles in three days, it was like saying, "Let's have another baby," to a woman who just gave birth. Uh, give me a moment.

By the time I walked into my office on Monday morning with my blisters and flip-flops, I knew I could not walk away. The 3-Day hooked me.

FATE-INSPIRED MOMENT #2

The connection with Penny's sister-in-law

Why Keep Going?

I HAD NO PLANS beyond walking that first Walk in 2003. Now, over two decades later, this much older lady is still walking. The question is why. Yes, it started with the vital need of raising funds for breast cancer research and support services. But it became more than that. The 3-Day Walk shaped my identity of who I am and who I hope to become.

Let's Get Physical

The San Diego event has a well-earned reputation of being one of the most challenging. The reason is the portion of the route with the so-called "hills." Starting with Torrey Pines, walkers climb an elevation of 1,100-plus feet that seems to go on forever. That portion of the route is where I nicknamed myself Captain Caboose.

A few years into the 3-Day, I took over as the captain for our team. We expanded to sixteen team members and most of my teammates are hikers. As a non-hiker, I soon discovered that my teammates tackled the elevation by powering up the hills like mountain goats bounding up to the top. My approach was a tad different.

Being one of the shortest team members (5 foot 3 inches), my pace was considerably slower. Not to mention, I was nowhere near the shape of my teammates.

At the bottom of the hills, I would instruct my hiker teammates to fly and I would take up the rear, like the caboose on a train. The early days saw me huffing and puffing my way to the top. That plus the mere challenge of walking twenty miles a day made it tough not to focus on the physical side of the Walk.

The event's training guide mapped out a plan for starting small, gradually building up to fifteen-to twenty-mile training walks. In the beginning, I followed it religiously. I soon entered the Mystery of the Feet.

In the first few years of following the training guide, I had no problem successfully completing it. Then the Walk happened. I would get about halfway through when the blisters bloomed. On my heels, on my toes, on both feet, they did not discriminate.

Throwing my feet over the side of the bed in the morning, the blood rushed to each bloated blister. The immediate pain was like a taser shot as my poor feet screamed in horror. I have always had sensitive feet, and they were not liking this one bit.

It was all out war. I tried thick socks, thin socks, and the sure-fire two socks. I slathered my feet in anti-blister balm and a mother's savior, Vaseline. It did not matter. The blisters were winning the war – until I rocked a new pair of shoes.

Rocky Adjustment

In addition to blister blowouts, I had toenails abandoning ship from all the pavement pounding. I lost both big toenails (one of them twice) and that baby toenail ripped from its home. I had to find a solution.

In 1996, a Swiss engineer Karl Müller, invented a new type of shoe nicknamed MBTs. The name is an acronym for Masai Barefoot Technology. The design mimicked the feeling of walking barefoot in sand, which Müller believed relieved stress on the back and other parts of the body.

The thick, curved sole created a funny-looking shoe. I decided I would add MBTs to my war against blisters. Walking in MBTs is like crossing a rocking boat – drunk. An old lady in MBTs. What could go wrong?

In 2006, despite planning on purchasing the sandal version, I allowed a salesperson to talk me into the closed shoe. The shoes eliminated the blisters, but I still lost a toenail. Lesson to self – do not let anyone dictate what is best for your feet!

The next year I purchased the sandals and it's been nirvana ever since. No blisters, no lost toenails – just happy feet. Well, as happy as feet can be walking sixty miles.

Getting Personal

My sister was the inspiration that got me started with the Walk. Unfortunately, the more Walks I completed, the more people I encountered who had breast cancer. I'm not sure if prior to my sister's diagnosis, I was simply unaware of its impact. The 3-Day changed that.

After completing that first Walk, I decided in 2004 to sign up as a crew member instead of a walker. I hated asking people for money and as a crew member, the event only required a minimal amount of funds.

I was looking forward to seeing Penny, Suzanne, and Diane again. At the end of the first Walk, I had asked Penny to put her contact information on the back of one of my business cards. Then I promptly misplaced it. Oh well, I was certain I would see them. I was working at the second pit stop and they were sure to come through there.

The three days passed, and I was disappointed that my newly found spirit sisters were not there. Shortly after the 2004 3-Day ended, I received an email from a client. She told me she found a person's name and address on the back of my business card.

My client had found Penny's contact information! She emailed me the information, so I pulled out a Christmas card to write Penny. Turns out, there was a startling reason Penny, Suzanne, and Diane had not participated in the 2004 Walk. Penny was diagnosed with breast cancer.

As the years have gone on, our team has dwindled to two walkers – Penny and me. Penny first invited me to join their team, and Penny is still inspiring this old lady to keep walking.

FATE-INSPIRED MOMENT #3

My client's discovery of Penny's missing contact information.

Another Linda in my life (not Penny's sister-in-law) has been a good friend for over forty years. In 2014, Linda developed breast cancer. Linda's diagnosis was another one of those fate-inspired moments.

After moving from San Diego in 2009, I return every year for the Walk, taking vacation time before the Walk starts. I stay with Linda until the day before the Walk when my teammates and I move into a rented house.

Normally, I only see Linda in November. But that year, I attended a client's Wellness Symposium that took place in June. Days before I arrived, Linda learned of her breast cancer diagnosis. If not for my San Diego-based client, I would have received another dreaded long-distance phone call about someone close to me who had breast cancer.

Both Linda's mother and sister had a history of breast cancer, first in one breast, then the other about a year later. Because of her mom's and sister's bilateral breast cancer, Linda was concerned about her own diagnosis. She wanted to discuss a bilateral mastectomy with her physician.

I was there when Linda told me about her discussion with the physician. He was adamantly opposed to the bilateral surgery. When Linda pushed him about her family history, his response was, "Your mother and sister were just incredibly unlucky."

Seriously? That's all it took for Linda to change physicians. Fortunately, she ended up with a great team and is cancer-free 11 years later. When Linda had the double mastectomy, her surgeon told her they found pre-cancerous cells in her other breast. Thank goodness Linda stood up for herself.

As I was getting ready to move into the rental with my teammates, Linda told me how glad she was that I was with her during that tough time. I was thankful I could be there, as I regretted being so far away from my sister when she received her diagnosis.

FATE-INSPIRED MOMENT #4

Having a client commitment to be in San Diego when my friend received her breast cancer diagnosis.

Right before the pandemic hit, my niece, Renee, was also diagnosed with breast cancer. First, my sister, then my teammate, Penny, then my friend, Linda, and now my niece. Additional teammates and I have had other forms of cancer, as well as multiple family members of mine.

Stop. Please stop.

So, I keep going, despite the blisters and toenails that decided they had enough. I ignore an aging body with its regular newsflashes that I am not the athlete I once was. I keep going for one simple reason.

Cancer is not done yet so neither am I.

Beyond Physical

Focusing on the physical side of the Walk is a common response. Some days it is all walkers can think about. I never would have believed that the sight of porta-potties lined up like a welcoming blue wall of relief would bring so much joy.

Although the event hosts multiple locations across the country, I have only participated in the San Diego event with all its demanding hills. But in 2012, my participation in this event was tested in a most unexpected way.

Susan G. Komen announced it would stop funding to Planned Parenthood due to a new policy Komen had adopted. That policy barred grants for organizations under investigation by local, state, or federal authorities.

During that time, a Florida representative launched a congressional investigation against Planned Parenthood to determine if the organization used taxpayer money to fund abortion services. Komen's announcement ignited a backlash that put Komen smack dab in the middle of the political debate.

Each year, walkers must raise a specified minimum in donations to participate in a 3-Day event. As walkers in the 3-Day, my teammates and I faced questions and outrage from some of our supporters who had contributed to our past Walks. As a result of the announcement, we lost supporters.

The following section is adapted from a blog post I wrote in 2012 when all of this was unfolding.

Bigger Than Money or Politics

by Cathy Miller| February 3, 2012| oldladybiz.com

The 3-Day/Planned Parenthood conflict left me aching with an overwhelming sadness of a meaning lost. For me, the 3-Day Walk is bigger than money or politics. After eight years of participating, I reflected on what the event meant to me. The 3-Day, 60-Mile Walk for the Cure is about:

Challenging yourself to achieve something you never dreamed possible.

Demonstrating your support in the most visible way you know how for your sister, your aunt, your niece, your teammates, and all those affected by cancer.

Sharing the experience with others who are hurting, healing, and reaching out. Developing friendships from those who extend a hand to become your teammates, who help pick you up when your spirit is lagging and who embrace you when all seems lost.

Providing hope to a pink-wigged crew member thanking a field of walkers as she tells us her cancer has metastasized, and you understand she is but one symbol of why you walk 60 miles in 3 days.

Loss when that crew member is no longer there, or another person has lost their battle against cancer.

Recognition that this is bigger than all of us. Certainly, bigger than money or politics.

No, it was not about supporting this side or that or placing blame. It was about a meaning lost. And that made me incredibly sad.

I have never been a fan of politics. At the time this occurred, political views had not crept into every strand of our lives. Not like it has today. I really hated that politics barged into something I treasured for everything that is good about people.

Anti-abortion groups targeted Komen since it started providing funds to Planned Parenthood. Komen allocated grants to Planned Parenthood for only clinical breast exams and mammogram referrals, but pro-life groups demanded Komen sever ties with Planned Parenthood.

The public relations nightmare the controversy created was devastating. The sister who made that promise by founding the organization, Nancy Brinker, stepped down as CEO and moved into a new role. Elizabeth Thompson, the president at the time, left the organization. Ultimately, Komen reversed its defunding decision and continued grants to Planned Parenthood.

Because I hated all things politics, I did not initially follow what was going on and was unaware of the applied pressures. My focus was on walking to help stomp out breast cancer.

But as I wrote in 2012, what was saddest to me was the meaning lost of why we walk sixty miles in three days. Each 3-Day participant has their own meaningful reason for walking or crewing. And it has nothing to do with politics.

My teammates and I grappled with what we wanted to do. Although none of my teammates stopped participating, plenty of other walkers did.

My decision was not easy. I decided I would keep going for all of those who could not and help make the future more promising for those yet to come.

CATHY MILLER

I recommitted to walking sixty miles in three days, one step at a time, as long as my body would allow.

PART TWO

BUMPING INTO BIAS

Old Lady Biz Publishing

BUMPING INTO BIAS

IN OVER TWO DECADES of participating in this event, I have met a lot of people. Each encounter became an important part of how I view the world we live in. Built-in biases (some I did not believe I had) challenged who I thought I was and who I hoped I'd be.

Biases are like a comfortable pair of jeans. We slip into them without thinking about trying a different look. I walked by that mirror for years without looking.

The built-in biases we direct at ourselves are the most damaging and are often the reason we treat ourselves and others the way we do. The 3-Day event helped me see that. It took decades of extreme walking for this self-proclaimed Pollyanna to recognize even people who want to do good have built-in biases.

> *In Eleanor Porter's novel (and later a film adaptation), Pollyanna was the main character, an orphan who brought unwavering optimism to every person she met. Excessive optimism is sometimes known as Pollyanna Syndrome or Pollyanna Principle. I can think of worse afflictions.*

Self-Inflicted Pain

We all do it. Slap labels on people and personalities. And as much as I hate labels, I apply several to myself – old lady, boomer, middle child of seven. Heck, I made a new brand out of Old Lady.

Even the labels applied to the challenge of breast cancer mean something different to those affected by the disease.

One of my friends and former coworkers, Sharlene, shared her perspective as a breast cancer survivor. On the news that Olivia Newton John had died from breast cancer, Sharlene wrote:

"...fight the urge to say, "she lost her battle with breast cancer." She didn't lose - the treatment failed."

How many times had I used the phrase, "lost her fight against breast cancer?" I used it in my blog post about the Planned Parenthood controversy.

Perspective is everything. I appreciate Sharlene sharing her viewpoint from a breast cancer survivor perspective, as well as her admonishment to:

"...spend more money on stage 4 BC treatment and less money on rah rah ads about getting mammograms and wearing pink!"

Dumped in Del Mar

I do like to poke fun at myself. But some of those labels said with a wink became defining in a way I had not anticipated.

In 2008, my teammates decided to try a new city for the 3-Day. At the time, I was the only southern California team member. The rest all lived in the San Francisco Bay area. The team decided to walk in their hometown area for a different experience. I was all up for it, until I injured my hip.

The San Francisco Walk took place in September. Fortunately, I learned that I could transfer my raised funds from that Walk to the San Diego Walk in November. So, I flew up to San Francisco to cheer on my teammates and then walked solo in San Diego.

But remember the first truth of the 3-Day. You never walk alone.

I hooked up with two other walkers at the opening ceremony in Del Mar. Chatting along the way, I made snarky references to my old body and said, "I'm fifty-seven," expecting a surprised, impressed response. That's not what I got.

Instead, one of my new walking partners responded in a disdainful tone, "I'm fifty-five." I realized my chatter had been extremely negative. But then I was not in a good place. I was in the waning days of a corporate career that had me stressed to the max and severely overweight.

At the first pit stop, we made our way to the revered porta-potties. We had arranged to meet at a specific spot to continue our walk. I stood at the meeting spot for several minutes when it hit me. My new walking partners dumped the fat, old, negative lady. All I could think was who can blame them?

Built-in stereotypes had done me in. My skewed definition of "old" was not my short-term walking partner's definition. This old lady who also recently entered fat girl status had erected a steeper barrier than the worst San Diego hill.

My self-esteem deflated like a tire with a slow leak. I completed the Walk, and joined various walkers for sections of the route, but I shied away from anything more than that.

Throughout my corporate career I interacted with clients. I loved meeting new people and was totally comfortable doing so. Yet here I was avoiding linking up with new walkers for fear of being hurt and spiraling down into that pit I created. Had I hit rock bottom?

An Unhappy Path

I was in reasonably good shape when I started the 3-Day in 2003. Where had that person gone over the next five years? Before the 2008 Walk my corporate boss said something to me that shook my world.

"You seem so unhappy, right down to your soul."

I knew that was not who I wanted to be. I had always been a positive person. I thrived in my work, but I was drowning in a body symbolically crying out for help.

I labored more than ever to complete the 3-Day Walk. My feet may have been blister-free, but the internal struggle latched on to its unhealthy exterior to make even the slightest incline breath-stealing. My conversations became peppered with self-doubt, even in my job that once was my whole identity.

My teammates never judged me, but I hated that I stood out like a puffer fish swimming in a sea of sleek, athletic dolphins.

Teammate and breast cancer survivor, Martina, generously purchased team shirts every year. I detested ordering a large and wearing a short-sleeve t-shirt under the cute tank top Martina chose one year. Just so I could hide my fat, flabby arms.

I still have flabby arms, but my attitude has changed. I don't care about my wingspan. Is that due to my 3-Day self-examination or a product of getting older? Either way, I know there are worse things in life than arms that wave goodbye all on their own.

Maybe those new walking partners did not dump me in Del Mar. Maybe that was me projecting my insecure self. Regardless, it was the first step back to me.

I thought back to when I felt my happiest, shortly before 2003 when I moved back to San Diego. My slim body reflected my happiness, but my weight was a manifestation of that, not the reason.

I took time to notice my surroundings and appreciate the inherent beauty in nature and in others. Frequent walks flipped my gray world to technicolor. When had the grass been that green, the ocean so blue?

I had better recognition of the built-in biases we all carry around with us. I was the me I wanted to be – more positive, kind, and caring. Somewhere along the way, I lost that.

Now, despite being back in the city I loved, I was not happy. Burying my feelings with too much food and too much wine, I spiraled downward. I knew I needed something big to pull me from the pit I created.

I was tired of my negativity with its giant scoop of insecurity. I was tired of me. I knew I could do better, and it was way past time I tried.

Walking Away

After struggling through the 2008 Walk, I took that giant leap. At the end of another long, stressful day at work, the desperate soul inside my fat shell quit on the spot. I left my long corporate career behind and started my own freelance business writing services.

It was not easy. Nor was it the most strategic time to walk away – we were right in the middle of the Great Recession of 2008. But thank God I did. It was lifesaving and the 3-Day Walk played a big role in my recovery.

In 2009, I left my cherished San Diego to move in with Mom in Boise, Idaho. She had been living alone since my dad passed and the house with an acre of land was too much to manage. Fortunately, my freelancing allowed me the flexibility to work anywhere.

I arrived on Mom's doorstep, an emotional and physical wreck. A new career and a new home were just the beginning toward recapturing a better me.

The road back took years and is a constant battle to maintain. In today's tough, angry world, it is exceedingly easy to fall off track. The 3-Day event helps me refocus and feel the peace of a better me.

Seven Cognitive Biases

THINK ABOUT ALL WE deal with. Work deadlines, family issues, and a tsunami of things to do. Who wouldn't want a way to manage all that stuff?

Positive Psychology defines cognitive bias as a pattern of thinking we adopt as a "mental shortcut" to cope with people or circumstances. It's a quick way to survive the overload of information that assaults our poor brains daily. As a result, we develop assumptions about people and similar incidents. When you walk sixty miles in three days, you have plenty of time to bump up against a few faulty assumptions.

The smarter-than-me people who study these mental shortcuts have identified hundreds of biases. Cognitive bias is the most common. I walked into the following seven types of cognitive biases in my two-plus decades of participating in the 3-Day event.

#1 – Stereotypes

Stereotypes are a type of cognitive bias involving generalizations made about groups of people. Often those generalizations are based on limited or inaccurate information. Like the ones we make about fat, old, negative people.

My mom had doubts about me attempting such an outrageous stunt as walking sixty miles in three days. First, it was my age. Later, her concern was a motherly one, fearing her fat, out-of-shape daughter would have a heart attack during the event.

Certainly, it was not an impossible outcome. I admit I had my own worries about the possibility. But when she saw the in-shape, healthy daughter returning, my mom became one of my biggest supporters.

Stereotypes run deep. The worst ones are the ones we tell ourselves. I beat myself up a lot in what I call the Fat Years of this event. I silently groaned when I saw even the slightest incline in the route. I hated not being able to keep up with my fit teammates. And I loathed the idea of getting on a sweep van.

Sweep vans are a fun part of the 3-Day. Crew members decorate vans in clever themes, like the Pimp Mobile that "picks up street walkers." If a walker is injured or just needs a break, the sweep vans swoop in and pick them up. The costumed crew take walkers to the next pit stop, lunch spot, or into camp. Medics are also available throughout the Walk.

During one of my Fat Years Walks, I struggled from the very start. Even walking up the slight incline of the driveway that led out of the Opening Ceremony at the Del Mar Fairgrounds had my breath sputtering like an engine with a combustion problem. Before I hit the first pit stop, my breath meter was teetering on empty.

I knew my out-of-shape body demanded I take a sweep van before attempting the long, arduous climb of Torrey Pines. I felt embarrassed and disgusted with myself. One coworker turned the knife in the open wound by saying she should have a refund on her donation because I didn't walk Torrey Pines. It did not matter that she said she was kidding. It hurt.

Linking walkers who get swept by the vans as failures because they did not walk all sixty miles is a worse stereotype than my fat girl stereotype. Are you a loser if you walk fifty-seven miles instead of sixty? Or twenty, thirty, or forty miles? I did not believe that about the walkers who used the sweep vans. Why did I believe it about myself?

A few years after I had walked myself to a healthier body, a teammate and I came upon a walker who was struggling. It was Day Three and there was one last, killer hill. The walker had pulled an inner thigh muscle. She was also significantly overweight.

She was determined to go up that nasty hill. I tried everything in my power to urge her to get on a sweep van. She was even more determined to walk the hill. Suddenly it hit me. This was me a few short years ago. Who was I to discourage this walker?

When I ripped off my baby toenail, I refused to be swept. Years before, I had been that fat girl, fighting the need to get in a sweep van. Yet, here I was, acting like I knew better. I assumed my situation trumped hers.

The determined walker and I parted ways when my team stopped at a wonderful Mexican restaurant for lunch, located at the base of the final hill. I invited her to join us, but she was going to tackle the hill instead.

I wished her well and told her I knew she could do it. No more pushing her to get on a sweep van. I believed in her. And you know what? She did it!

I was thrilled when I saw the walker at the Closing ceremony (fate steps in again?) I asked her how she did. When she told me she made it up the hill, I hugged her and told her she was awesome.

The experience was an eye-opener. Stop judging others by my life.

#2 – Anchoring Bias

I like to think I have an open mind about people and circumstances. But my lifelong pursuit of keeping it simple has me tripping over some of my built-in biases – tripping is not a word you want associated with walking sixty miles.

All the data banging around in my head fries my boomer brain. Thank the memory gods for my electronic brain (or maybe I should thank Steve Jobs). With so many details, it's easy to latch onto an idea and hang on. The bias buffs call that an anchoring bias.

When I became our team captain, I discovered there were a lot of details to manage. Housing for the team, transportation while in San Diego, event deadlines for signing up and raising required funds, to name a few.

After spending over three decades in the corporate world, I knew some people were detail-oriented and others were not. That was okay with me. I would adapt to the person's style.

My teammate, Penny, did not always answer my team emails, mostly letting her office manager deal with them. I latched on to the idea that Penny was not a details-person. Talk about wrong!

On our tenth anniversary as a team, we had a reunion at a teammate's beautiful Lake Tahoe home. I stayed with Penny in the Bay area, and we drove together to Lake Tahoe. On the way back to the airport, Penny asked if I'd mind if we stopped at one of her job sites.

Penny owns her own interior design company. As an avid HGTV aficionado, I was excited to see Penny on the job. It did not take long for me to marvel at all the details Penny juggled with contractors, the client, and retailers.

She answered multiple design questions for the contractors, sent the client a picture of a rug Penny thought would be a perfect addition, and followed up on a delayed order with one of the retailers – all within fifteen minutes of arriving onsite. How did I ever think Penny was not a details person?

I laughed with Penny about it, telling her she simply did not have room in her brain for 3-Day trivia. Isn't it amazing how often we learn something about a longtime friend that knocks us off our biased beliefs?

#3 – Bandwagon Bias

Bandwagon in this context is not one of the sweep vans, although that could have been a good addition to the pit stop I worked in 2004. We were known as the Wild, Wild Breast Saloon.

Bandwagon bias is when a person "adopts certain behaviors, style, or attitudes simply because everyone else is doing it." That type of bias has never sat well with me because of my lifelong affliction with Middle Child of Seven Syndrome.

My mom and dad had seven children. I was right in the middle as the fourth oldest and the fourth youngest. Sprinkle in the Miller stubbornness and being told what to do becomes the gasoline to my flame of resistance.

There is no shortage of advice for the 3-Day regarding what you should wear, how you should train, or when you should get on a sweep van. I love hearing from other walkers or crew members about what worked for them. I am happy to try out their suggestions.

But throw in the phrase, *EVERYONE does it this way* and prepare to meet my version of the Incredible Hulk. Practice what you preach, right? Obviously, I failed in that department when I tried to force that walker onto a sweep van.

Remember my funny-looking MBTs sandals? Several walkers criticized my choice because the curved bottom increases the amount of energy I expend while walking. But when the alternative is lost toenails and a burst of blisters, the extra energy is more than worth it. For me. And that's the key. My shoe of choice may not be yours but that's okay. You do you.

#4 – Confirmation Bias

Confirmation bias can hitch a ride on the bandwagon express when the information confirms what a person already believes. One example involved the event's training guide.

A walker expressed worry over not having followed the guide as closely as she had in the past. When she got blisters, she swore it was because she had not followed the plan. Maybe it was, but it could have been some other factor, like shoes, or socks, or a change in her stride. But in that walker's mind, the blisters confirmed her belief that the sporadic training caused the problem.

During my fat year when I rode the sweep van, I remember one walker who expressed to her fellow walkers, "I don't believe anyone walks all sixty miles." Those sitting next to her nodded their heads in agreement.

For once, I kept my mouth shut. I knew that statement was not true. This was the first year I got on the van. This fat girl had walked all sixty miles every year except for that one. And my athletic teammates sure as heck walked all sixty miles.

I suspect if I had spoken up, that walker would have dismissed the idea that many walkers completed all sixty miles. Her confirmation bias needed to believe the opposite.

#5 – Implicit Bias

I will never forget a story I heard on my first 3-Day Walk. As we wound toward the center of Del Mar, I saw two teenaged girls walking. Each wore a strapless, ankle-length prom dress in a deep pink color.

What walkers wear while walking sixty miles boggles my mind. But this look was astounding, and I knew I needed to hear their story. I was surprised to learn why the two girls were wearing prom dresses.

The girls were sixteen years old, the minimum age to participate. One of the girls played volleyball in high school. One day she noticed a lump on one of her breasts. She scheduled a doctor's appointment, but the doctor told her she probably got hit with the volleyball and not to worry about it. Fortunately, the girl's mother did not accept that answer.

After pursuing the problem further, mother and daughter learned the sixteen-year-old had breast cancer. Wait. What? Sixteen-year-olds don't get breast cancer. That is what the first physician believed. He was a victim of implicit bias.

Implicit bias leads to an unconscious assumption based on factors such as gender, race, health status, and other characteristics. The bias exists deep in the subconscious and is often shaped by experience.

In healthcare, implicit bias can lead to inaccurate diagnosis or treatment. Linda's first physician who described her family history as "incredibly unlucky" had his own dose of implicit bias.

A sixteen-year-old with breast cancer is rare (less than 1% of all cases occur in individuals under twenty years of age). But those who are diagnosed with breast cancer tend to have more aggressive forms and lower survival rates when compared to older individuals.

This beautiful teenager had missed her prom due to breast cancer, so she and her best friend decided to wear bright pink dresses while walking sixty miles in three days. I saw them all three days, still walking in their pink prom dresses. Unbelievable. I often wonder how she is doing today.

The rarity of the disease in young people is little comfort when diagnosed. Just ask the twenty-plus Young Survivors Coalition who gather on Day Three of the event to greet walkers. If ever there was a symbol of why we walk, this line of beautiful young survivors is it.

Another implicit bias error is thinking breast cancer only affects women. About 2,800 men in the U.S. are diagnosed with breast cancer each year. While living in San Diego, my morning started with coffee and watching my favorite news anchors on ABC Channel 10. In 2004, one of the anchors, Bill Griffith, shared he had been diagnosed with breast cancer.

Thirteen months earlier when Bill questioned his physician about the painful lump, he was told, "Men don't get breast cancer." Even the specialist Bill's physician reluctantly referred him to said the same thing – men don't get breast cancer.

Another implicit bias proven wrong. Few false assumptions have the potential for such deadly consequences.

#6 – Self-serving Bias

My decades-long walk through the 3-Day event was often a search for self-esteem. We all want to feel good about ourselves, but life has a way of beating us down. A self-serving bias creeps in as a defense mechanism against more pain.

Self-serving bias assumes good things occur because of something we did. The bad things are someone else's fault or due to circumstances beyond our control. My Fat Years were due to a stressful corporate environment. It was the job's fault. I remember another incident where I placed blame for my bad behavior on someone else.

My teammate, Kristin, and I shared a few 3-Day Walks. In 2017, we were driving back to the house we rented for the weekend. The house had a lockbox with an extra key in it. I forgot to put the spare key in the lockbox. I found that out when one teammate flew in later and was trying to access the house.

Kristin became worried that I may not remember to put the key in the next day. She had to fly out immediately following the Walk as she was on call at the hospital where she worked as a pediatrician.

"I need to be sure I can get in, so I don't miss my flight," Kristin said.

I am sure she did not expect my response. With my head spinning in true Exorcist form, I angrily replied, "What am I? Twelve? I will put the key in the lockbox!"

What Kristin did not know was I had a relationship with a person who always blamed me any time anything went wrong. I became a handy target as that person was intent on not being the one at fault – no matter how mundane the problem.

Psychologists call that projection. It is a self-serving comfort used to attribute an individual's own negative traits or behaviors on someone else. Now I was projecting my aggressive response and silently blaming the person who did the same to me.

My pent-up frustration blew up all over Kristin. As much as I hated being blamed for *everything*, I attacked Kristin for something I did. I was the one who forgot to put the key in the lockbox. Time to put on my big girl pants and take ownership.

After the haze of anger left me, I apologized (multiple times) to Kristin – even months later. Ah, Catholic guilt.

#7 – In-group Bias

In-group bias supports internal group members while rejecting or alienating outsiders. I know I tended to resist adding team members we did not know. Not a good look for the captain.

Meeting my teammates is one of the biggest blessings of participating in this event. When I met Penny, Suzanne, and Diane on my first Walk, I had no idea how much we would grow as a group of walkers. We walked for years before we decided we needed a team name.

In 2006, we took inspiration from two adorable, little girls who were standing in the back of a pickup parked along the route. They were holding a sign they made themselves.

Fight like a Girl!

Loved it! That became our team's name through 2012 until some clever(?) person trademarked the phrase. After celebrating our 10-year anniversary in beautiful Lake Tahoe, we changed our team's name to the Pink Tahoe Ladies.

From our initial meeting to today, our team gradually grew to sixteen members. Some walked one Walk, others walked several. Each one of them walked into my heart.

I am the oldest (so what else is new?). At times, I was forty years older than my youngest teammate. Our team has daughters, nieces, and sisters of other teammates. We are our own special family.

Each team member connects directly or indirectly to at least one of our original group members of Penny, Diane, Suzanne, and me.

Penny's Connections

LAUREN is Penny's daughter. Lauren was only nineteen years-old when she signed up in 2011. I called Lauren the sparkle of the team. She injected this old lady with so much light and energy.

In 2017, Lauren moved to Hawaii where she followed in her mother's (and grandmother's) footsteps into interior design. My little sparkle successfully runs her own design company. I could not be prouder.

JAMIE is Penny's niece (and Lauren's cousin). I have not walked with Jamie, but she was on the San Francisco team I cheered for in 2011 when the team walked for the second time in the city.

I was impressed with Jamie's giving nature and quiet strength, especially for someone so young. Now, Jamie is a mom of two adorable children. You know you're getting older when the youngest members of the team are having babies.

JANA and Penny met when their daughters were campfire girls. Jana is another team member who walked the San Francisco Walks, as well as one in Arizona in 2009. I missed Arizona, so we did not walk together.

After meeting Jana in San Francisco, I got to know her even better through her personal blog. She is a gifted writer and children's advocate who recently published a children's book. I love Jana's spiritual, healing sense she brings to our tumultuous world.

HOLLY is also a friend of Penny's. They originally met through Penny's work as an interior designer. When Holly first walked, she was living in Connecticut and walked in 2014 and 2016 in San Diego.

Holly is a shot of vitality and laugh-out-loud fun that helps make those sixty miles fly by. Born in Canada, Holly is the perfect example of why I love the people of Canada. They are the loyal friends you hope to have.

JENN worked for Penny's husband at one time, and along with Jenn's husband, the four of them socialized together. Jenn first walked the 2008 San Francisco Walk, then San Diego in 2011 and 2014.

The trait I love most about Jenn is, at 4 foot-something, she is shorter than I am. Finally, someone without a long stride! Jenn also used to sport the worst blisters I have ever seen. Removing her sock, her blisters looked like an overfilled water balloon just waiting to pop. Despite the pain (she never complained about), Jenn finished every Walk. Our small but mighty warrior.

As I mentioned, Dianne and Suzanne are sisters, so they share multiple teammate connections.

Diane's Connections

KRISTIN is Diane's daughter (Suzanne's niece). Kristin and I walked together early in my 3-Day experience in 2007. At the time, Kristin was the youngest team member at age twenty-three, but an age considered old to be applying to medical school.

Kristin's unrelenting pursuit of her dream captivated me. She achieved her medical degree and is now practicing as a pediatrician. While attending medical school in Michigan, Kristin walked the Michigan 2013 3-Day Walk. Don't mess with Kristin's fierce determination.

MICHELLE is Diane's (and Suzanne's) niece. She joined our 2005 San Diego team when Diane was unable to do so due to back problems. Michelle wanted so much to be a mom and in the following year she did just that!

It has been so fun watching this beautiful, strong woman thrive in her role as mother to her amazing daughter (who celebrated her eighteenth birthday last year). You know this aging thing could get depressing if it didn't bring so many happy outcomes.

Suzanne's Connections

JULIE worked out at the same gym as Suzanne, and they soon became fast friends. Julie joined our San Diego team in 2006 when Michelle used the pregnancy excuse not to walk. Julie is a beautiful ball of friendship and love.

I always smile when I think about us trudging along during the Walk when we came across someone offering Starbucks coffee. Julie took a few sips, jumped in the air shouting, "Wahoo," while kicking her feet in opposite directions. I can't walk with coffee without spilling it all over me, much less leap in the air. I guess we each have our own special talents.

MARTINA also worked out at the same gym as Suzanne and Julie. She became the third breast cancer survivor on our team, diagnosed at the astonishingly young age of 24.

Her first 3-Day event was in San Francisco, but she also walked San Diego in multiple years. Martina is one of the most generous, life-loving people I have ever met. She is always up for an adventure and merry mischief.

As a breast cancer survivor, Martina gives back as the program coordinator of a non-profit that provides free wigs to women experiencing hair loss from chemotherapy or other causes.

BETH is Martina's friend and former college sorority sister. Beth's first Walk was the Year of the Monsoon in 2010. And yet she came back for four more Walks. Not surprising as Beth, who was a personal trainer at the time, is one of the most fit people I know – not that I tend to hang out with scores of remarkably buffed people. Beth had no problem rocking those team tank tops Martina gave our team.

I remember one Walk where Beth stretched at one of the pit stops by doing pushups. I hid safely behind my camera and took pictures. Today, Beth is bringing her positive energy to her new role as life coach, author, and speaker.

KELLEN is Martina's oldest daughter, who joined us in San Diego in 2016, 2017, and 2018. Despite being a HUGE Notre Dame (ND) fan, I still love Kellen who at the time was attending the University of Southern California (USC), a big ND rival.

Kellen went on to become a teacher, get married, and have a beautiful son. While writing this book, I learned Kellen and Dean are expecting their second child, a girl! I wonder if I'll still be walking when Kellen's daughter (and son!) are old enough to join us.

My Connections

ABBY is a friend and former coworker of mine. She joined our team the same year as Beth in 2010. But she had walked the year before with another team, until she came to her senses and joined ours.

In my corporate days, Abby and I traveled frequently for work. You get to know a lot about a person when you're sitting in a plane or rental car for hours. I don't think I've ever seen Abby mad. When I think of Abby, I think calm, soft-spoken, and peaceful. Lord knows we can all use an Abby in our lives. Abby is currently living in Australia and embracing the whole adventure as only Abby can.

That's our Pink Tahoe Ladies team – so far. I never close the book on new team members. However, when you have a well-connected group like our team, you run the risk of developing that in-group bias. I learned that lesson when I heard Abby's story about her experience with her prior team.

Outside the In-Group

As I mentioned, Abby had walked with a different team in 2009 before joining ours. Her younger teammates were the first ones out of camp at the start of each day. They walked at a pace to ensure being among the top finishers, which was important to the group.

Abby could not keep up, nor did she try. Abby walked at her own pace, which I loved about her. Abby had found the team online at the event's site where she clicked on a link to join their team. During the Walk, the team captain told Abby that they would have to leave her behind as she could not keep up. Hearing her story, my Catholic guilt immediately kicked in about my own in-group bias.

Abby told us how much she appreciated a vastly different experience compared to the prior team. It helped to have a slow-moving Captain Caboose on her team. Chug along with me.

I wondered why her previous team was open to new members when they clearly had such an in-group bias for speed. They obviously had not heard the event's repeated statement that the 3-Day Walk is not a race.

PART THREE

A JOURNEY OF THE HEART

Old Lady Biz Publishing

A JOURNEY OF THE HEART

> "If you laugh, you think, and you cry, that's a full day. That's a heck of a day. You do that seven days a week, you're going to have something special."
> **Jim Valvano in his 1993 ESPYS speech**

MY JOURNEY STARTED WITH a shared promise to a sister. What it became was a destination. How could I not be changed with what I saw, what I heard, and what I experienced? And the journey is not done yet.

I laugh, I think, and I cry. The journey is something special. This path to a destination I have yet to reach gives me hope to be the best person I can be.

Throughout the decades of walking, I continue to try to follow three life lessons that guide me on my path – 1) Accept myself first, 2) appreciate the uniqueness of others, 3) change my narrative on unconscious bias. The following stories formed the early pages for my life lessons guide.

#1 – Accept Myself First

> "Bias is a process and builds over a lifetime."
> The Bias Inside Us, SI.edu

ONE OF THE THEME parks for LEGOLAND® is situated in northern San Diego County in the city of Carlsbad. I have always been fascinated by the creativity in Lego creations. Each block starts on its own, then gradually builds by connecting to other blocks.

Our built-in biases are like a Lego creation. It takes a slew of experiences and influences to develop our own bias creation. To understand and change my built-in biases, I started with me and the blocks that built them.

The Whole Package

When I ripped my infamous toenail off, I refused to be swept by a van even though it was the last pit stop. After helping me get on my feet, my teammate, Penny, grabbed my fanny pack, saying she would carry it for me.

"I will carry it," I stubbornly responded.

"It's okay, I'll carry it," Penny replied. Snatching it from Penny's hand, I gritted my teeth and said, "No, I've got it," bristling with righteousness.

I later thought, "Geez, what's the big deal?"

Asking for or accepting help has always been difficult for me. It still is. Yet, I love volunteering to help others. Psychologists refer to an unhealthy level of self-reliance as hyper-independence. Good to know that at my age I could be hyper at anything.

To get in touch with my built-in biases, I had to examine why I thought the way I did and how that influenced how I treated myself and others. It's not as easy as it sounds. Lucky for me, I have a heavy dose of that Catholic guilt I talked about.

Again, with nasty labels. But whatever it is causing me to feel guilty, at least it has me questioning my actions. I know better than to walk away from the answer.

Being the middle child of seven has interesting dynamics. Competing with so many siblings, I developed a stubborn, do-it-myself persona. But, as my oldest brother once said, I may have the tenderest hearts of any of them. I am easily hurt.

My sociable side loves being with people and I can get a bit animated and chatty. One friend told me she understood why I never did drugs – I never needed them to get high.

My alter ego seeks the quiet solitude of my own self. Before moving in with Mom, I lived alone most of my adult life. Unlike friends who told me they hated being alone, I reveled in it. I loved being able to do what I wanted or go where I chose, even if that meant escaping to my own home.

I confused more than one person with the loud, outgoing character they were used to who suddenly pulled the plug. Especially during my corporate road warrior days, my friends knew not to call me on Saturdays when I spent the day alone to recharge.

My chatty and quiet sides are my own version of yin yang. Taoism's philosophical beliefs views Yin Yang as a symbol of its "holistic view of reality."

> **The Yin and Yang principles act on one another, affect one another and keep one another in place.**
> **– Chuang Tzu**

The Yin-Yang philosophy recognizes my chatty and quiet sides as opposites but considers them interdependent and unable to exist separately.

I guess I must accept the whole package, however painful that may be. But understanding that is who I am helps me accept and find the balance to achieve harmony, yin-yang style.

Redefining Normal

Another product of my past is my environment. We know what we know. I remember when I first moved to California from the Midwest, where I was born and raised, I encountered so much outside my norm.

I always thought I came from a "normal" family – two parents (still married) – siblings – you know – normal. I told friends I decided my background was abnormal. I never met so many single-parent and blended families.

That's one of the great things about participating in the 3-Day event. You meet people from all over the world, from all types of background, and all different ages. All coming together because of one common goal. To kick cancer to the curb. Once and for all.

The demographics from the 2021 San Diego 3-Day Walk offer a perfect example of the diversity of this event.

> Walkers = 2,300, Crew = 250
> Youngest walker = 15 years old, oldest walker = 89 years old
> 360 men registered
> 500 survivors registered
> Over 800 first-time walkers registered
> Representation from every state (except Mississippi).
> Walkers also from France, the Virgin Islands, Puerto Rico, and Canada!

Accepting Help

Besides being known for its hills, the San Diego event is also known for its phenomenal community support. Dressed in costumes and all things pink, community members hold signs that are inspiring and laugh-out-loud funny.

A survivor's sign:
"People like you saved me."
A community supporter's sign:
"Why walk 60 miles? Because walking 61 miles would be silly."

Young children pass out stickers and bracelets and Mardi Gras-like beads. Dog owners dye their dogs pink. Others bake cookies and offer a Willy Wonka dream of mile after mile of chocolate and sugary treats.

I am thankful I do not have a sweet tooth. My teammates are stunned when I pass it all by, and my sweets-loving mother thinks I must be adopted. But the San Diego community offers so much more than sweet treats. Walkers share hugs, laughs, and tears with a community that understands.

As much as my independent-loving nature hates to admit it, I need that community to make it through all three days. Every year, lining the route and cheering us on, the community is like warm, fuzzy slippers on a chilly morning. They always show up, even during the 2010 downpour I call the Year of the Monsoon.

On Day Two that year, the heavens backed up along the route and dumped a truckload of rain. My teammates and I had purchased umbrellas at our favorite Mission Market, but Mother Nature had other ideas.

By the end of the day, strong winds snatched the frames and inverted umbrellas into tattered fragments begging for relief. My sandal-clad feet squished in protest as walkers plodded along, pelted by the driving rain as the wind set sail to our yellow ponchos. As bad as it was, no one expected community members to be out there. Yet, there they were. Huddled under their own umbrellas, cheering us on.

I may not like to ask for help, but I am eternally grateful to the San Diego community that gives it freely, especially when I need it most. Their support is just the lift I need to walk sixty miles in three days.

Humbled by Support

To participate each year, walkers must raise a minimum amount in donations to the cause. I wrestled with the idea of asking for money. It's that old mind block of asking for help.

In my corporate days, it was easier than I thought. During the latter days of my career, I was a licensed insurance broker. Some of the contributions came from insurance carriers hoping to get our referrals.

Being able to walk year after year was the focus for me, no matter what the motivation of the contributor was. But that viewpoint changed.

It was due to my fundraising that my eyes were opened to the devastating effect of cancer on so many lives. Not only did I learn the stories of 3-Day participants, but also the stories of those who generously donated.

One story hit my heart hard. I was in the final year of my corporate career. I met Tom, an insurance carrier representative, for the first time. As he stood in my office, he saw a sign I had in my office about the 3-Day. He asked me about it. When I explained about the event and my participation, he asked if he could contribute.

He hesitantly shared his story. I could tell it was not easy for him. He had been battling cancer for 12 years and was currently in remission. This brave, young man had shared something very personal, and my heart broke for his pain of remembrance.

I asked him if I could give him a hug. As we embraced, I knew I could never quit. He and all cancer survivors endured so much. As long as I was able, I would continue to walk sixty miles in three days.

I thought when I left my corporate days behind, I would have a difficult time raising the minimum required to walk. But my contributors never let me down. With their generous contributions, I easily raise the minimum. Some have been with me from the beginning. Others contribute after reading one of my posts. I should not be surprised but every year their generous response humbles me.

I suspect some of my longtime contributors continue to support me because they are amazed this Old Lady is still walking. So am I.

Busted Bias

The 3-Day Walk blew up my self-deprecating outlook about age. Not only did the Del Mar dumpers blast my age bias, but the number of 3-Day Walkers who are my age or older is astonishing.

No wonder they were not impressed that I started my first Walk at age fifty-one.

A 3-Day walker, Karen, asked herself what she could do for her sixtieth year of life. She decided to walk sixty miles in three days. Seems appropriate because (like the sign said) walking 61 miles would be silly.

She walked the full sixty miles for the first five Walks "until some sweet sweep van gals told me it was no shame to sweep." Karen caught on to this concept much faster than I did.

Seventeen years later, Karen is planning to walk the 2025 San Diego 3-Day. I hope to see her there.

Age-Proof

If you need further age-defying proof, meet 3-Day walker extraordinaire, George. George kicked any age bias in the butt when he started walking at age seventy. By seventy-five, he was walking every sponsored Walk. In those days, that was fourteen Walks!

Due to health issues, George retired at the age of ninety-one(!) with his last being the 2023 San Diego 3-Day Walk. I am grateful I was able to share one more George story with him right before I headed up the daunting Torrey Pines hill.

George walked for the love of his life. She had battled breast cancer for most of their married life. George told me how he laid down beside her on her final days. He said he wished he could go with her.

"George, you need to stay here because you have so much more to do," his loving wife said. A short time later, she took her last breath.

This beautiful man and his courageous wife exemplify everything you need to know about this event. I missed seeing George in 2024, but I know this age-defiant man is making this chaotic world a much better place. I love you, George.

Ageless Benny

Another age-buster is my dear friend, Benny. I met Benny in 2004 when I decided to crew instead of walking. Along with her best friend, Debbie, Benny was a 3-Day veteran. She and Debbie had walked the Avon Walks in their hometown of Seattle, Washington.

You may have heard, it rains a bit in Seattle. Debbie's feet were soaked, and she developed a serious infection. That was her last time participating as a walker. But that did not stop Benny and Debbie. They volunteered as crew members for the Susan G. Komen 3-Day in San Diego.

Debbie wore a different Miss Kitty outfit each of the three days for our Wild, Wild Breast Saloon pit stop. Benny and I armed ourselves with water pistols that helped cool off the sweaty walkers. Both Debbie and Benny are my age, yet as exhausting as crewing can be, these two inspired and energized me as a rookie crew member.

Sadly, we lost Debbie to Alzheimer's in 2016. But Benny continues her volunteering, expanding her event causes to include fundraising for Alzheimer's, as well as breast cancer and many other forms of cancer. Benny walks, runs, climbs stairs, and bicycles to help raise funds for these charitable causes.

This year Benny plans to participate in eight 5Ks, one stair climb, one bike ride, and another bike ride with a 5K tacked on. And she continues her streak of crewing at the San Diego 3-Day Walk.

Benny does this every dang year. When my old body starts nagging me, I think, what would Benny do? Then I do much less.

While my stubborn, independent streak still rears up, the 3-Day event has shown me we all need help. It could be someone diagnosed with breast cancer, the loved ones they left behind, or someone walking on their behalf.

If someone offers a hand, I take it. When I receive a compliment, I accept it and say thank you. When life does not go as planned, I learn and move on. Okay, mostly. I remain a work in progress.

I still poke fun at my age, but I know we are capable of utterly amazing things, far beyond what we ever thought possible. Just ask a cancer survivor.

Lesson #1 Learned: When I understand and accept myself, I am ready to receive and offer the best of me.

#2 – Appeciate Unique

COMING FROM A LARGE family like mine, I am fascinated by how each sibling is unique. We were basically raised the same, yet we have distinct differences. Maybe my mom and dad wore down by the time they got to their last child, particularly since there are seven of us.

Even in families, we build our own stereotypes. I've read a lot about family birth orders. My middle child status in the pecking order is believed to produce traits like independent (check), peacemaker (also check), and rebellious – say what? My parents would never describe me that way. But what about the outside world?

Johns Hopkins neuroscientist, David Linden, said in an interview with *Psychology Today* that while traits may prove true within the family, they do not automatically transfer to the outside world.

> *"...it's not as if first children who tend to be the leaders in their family are the leaders on the playground at school or the leaders of corporations. It doesn't transfer over that way."*
> **David Linden**

When I slam up against a built-in bias, I think about the assumptions made about a middle child that ignite my inner Hulk. Instead, I look for the uniqueness of an individual, even if that's family. And that means listening and appreciating their uniqueness.

Listen to Their Story

> *"When we listen to others' stories, we enter their worlds and see things through their eyes."*
> **Psychology Today**

Geography keeps my teammates and me apart for most of the year. But once a year we come together to share an event close to our heart. My teammate, Martina, once expressed that we knew more about her life than people she sees much more than once a year.

When you walk sixty miles in three days, you do a lot of talking. And if you do it right, you do even more listening. It's all about putting one foot in front of the other. One goal. No distractions. It's connecting in the truest, unbiased form.

We call this special place the Pink Bubble. I dread the time when I step outside the Pink Bubble and return to real life, but I try to take the best with me.

So many stories I have shared here, yet so many more to tell. Two-plus decades of images roll through my heart, wrapping me in hope.

Hope expressed by the ninety-year-old survivor shaking the hand of all 2,000-plus walkers. Hope by the moms walking so their kids know a life without cancer. Hope shared by life partners walking together to make a difference. Hope through friends and loved ones. So much hope.

How can you not be changed when you learn why a sixteen-year-old girl is walking in a vibrant pink prom dress? How can you not feel the commitment of a woman who rolled along the route in a wheelchair after breaking her foot? Or admire the other walkers who pushed her up those gnarly San Diego hills? Or cry along the Memorial Mile as you walk by the photos of loved ones lost to breast cancer?

The 3-Day event is a writer's dream of a buffet table stuffed with delectable and inspiring stories, waiting to be devoured. The more I listened, the more I learned about others and myself. Stereotypes and other built-in biases muffle the sound of those stories.

If I had not walked in the 3-Day events, I would have lost life-changing opportunities. So, I listen to their stories and live a changed life. Those stories help make me a better person.

Share their Story

"The courage it takes to share your story might be the very thing someone else needs to open their heart to hope."
— **Unknown**

Dealing with a breast cancer diagnosis takes incredible courage. But can you imagine stripping down to be essentially nude on national TV?

Courtney learned at age thirty-three that she had breast cancer. Thinking she was on her way back to a "normal" life, she had her world rocked again. At the age of thirty-five, the cancer was back. Even more shocking, Courtney learned she had a mutated BRACA-2 gene.

> **BRCA Gene**
> The Breast Cancer Gene-1 (BRCA-1) and The Breast Cancer Gene-2 (BRCA-2) help repair DNA damage. We all have two copies, one from each parent. But for some people, those genes may be damaged. In women, the damaged BRCA gene causes increased risk for breast and ovarian cancer.

Courtney had over twenty surgeries and a double mastectomy. The brutality of the disease and treatment left her with low esteem about her body. This beautiful warrior committed to making a difference by raising awareness and working with the Young Survivor Coalition.

Courtney knew she needed to start with herself; she found an unthinkable way to build her confidence while raising awareness about this disease. She stripped down on TV. Well, that's certainly one way to bring awareness.

Back in 2016, there was a show called Skin Wars, featuring body painters. The show had an unusual idea for honoring breast cancer survivors. The body painters used the chosen survivors' bodies as a canvas to paint them from head to toe. Going way "out of her comfort zone," Courtney applied for one of the spots and was surprised to be one of those selected.

Talk about courage. Courtney stood in front of cameras, "basically completely nude except for little nude underwear and pasties," her body painted to represent her story. The body painter depicted Courtney's fear of the cancer returning, the mutated gene, and this survivor's warrior status as a participant in fourteen 3-Day Walks. It was a life-changing moment for Courtney.

I first met Courtney through her Pink Wings business that sells commemorative pins for the 3-Day Walk. When I learned her story, I knew I had to share it. Like the other stories here, I am in awe of the overwhelming generosity of those sharing their stories of grit, perseverance, and survival.

Life is hard for all of us. By sharing their stories, I hope you, too, will find what you need to put one foot in front of the other and become a better person. For yourself first, then others.

Think Different

> *"I believe that every person is born with talent."*
> **Maya Angelou**

When I started my own business, I had to learn to stop acting like an employee and start thinking like a business owner. The Holy Grail of marketing is a unique selling proposition (USP).

If you want to stand out, you need to discover what is different about your business or your product. Yet, when it comes to human beings, we often shun those who are different from us. I don't get it. Do we really want a plain, boring world of clones? If you do, I am sure I lost you early in this book.

Throughout my business writing career, I developed what I call Miller Musings. The musings are my personal soundbites that express ideas for better communication. They work for both business and personal purposes because good communication is good communication. Isn't that profound?

So, I apply my Miller Musings to both my business and personal life. Like when I am told a concept is wrong, or this is the right way and the other way is wrong, I apply the following Miller Musing.

> *It's not right or wrong – just different.*
> **Miller Musing**

We judge the most inconsequential elements of life, like the clothes people wear or how they style their hair. We deride someone's height, weight, or the color of their skin. And many times, we do not know a single thing about that person.

The 3-Day event in its Pink Bubble world is a walk through quirky and different. Walkers, crew members, and staff have their own stories and outlook on life.

One of my favorite questions to ask a walker I just met is, "What made you decide to walk in the 3-Day?" Often the response is a who rather than what. Someone special to that person knocked into that frightening breast cancer diagnosis. Or the person I asked was the one knocked sideways.

But sometimes the answer is not who but why. In 2024, Penny and I met two male walkers, Curtis and Jeff. It was their first 3-Day Walk.

When we asked why they decided to participate, asking if it was for someone special, they said that they did not know anyone diagnosed with breast cancer. They simply wanted to do something for a good cause and landed on the 3-Day.

On the last day, Curtis gave Penny and me small bowls that had been broken and transformed using the Japanese art form, Kintsugi.

Kintsugi

All beautiful things carry distinctions of imperfection. Your wounds and imperfections are your beauty. Like Kintsugi, the Japanese art of mending broken pottery with gold, we are all perfectly imperfect. Breakage and mending are honest parts of a past which should not be hidden. Your wounds and healing are a part of your history; a part of who you are. Every beautiful thing is damaged. You are that beauty; we all are.
— Bryant McGill, Author (Facebook post, July 26, 2017)

Curtis included a note with his gift.

"May this bowl be a reminder of the strength and resilience you have within."
Curtis

Lord, I love this 3-Day event. It helps me "think different" about life and the people I meet. Like a broken bowl, I appreciate the perfectly imperfect individuality waiting to shine through.

My goal is to listen, and share, and appreciate the uniqueness of each person. I want to carry their life lessons with me wherever I go.

After all, humans are mysterious and intriguing, and everyone has a story to share. And for me, that makes life much more interesting than walking through fields of clones.

Lesson #2 Learned: The uniqueness of everyone is a gift waiting to be opened and shared.

#3 – Change Narrative

My built-in biases bully their way in when I am at my most vulnerable. Tired and stressed, that inner voice attempts a coup over the better me.

Two-plus decades of walking sixty miles in three days has put me on alert for those sneaky whisperings of a path I do not want to take. Sometimes the bias barges through but I try to tackle it before it takes over.

I change the narrative by talking to myself, those around me, and then walking the walk to a better me.

Talking to Myself

Day Two of the event has its own special "hill." It is the one I hate the most, even though it is the shortest of the three days.

Narragansett Street in Ocean Beach is a steep 545 feet of torture to my aging body. It is the toughest hill for me to accomplish my goal of walking it without stopping – although crawling may be a more accurate term.

In 2023, navigating Narragansett was even more grueling. I was experiencing a bad case of nausea. Forget about climbing my nemesis without stopping, I fought to complete it at all.

It's times like these when that annoying voice in my head hits me up with doubt, scorn, and constant urges to give up.

"*You're too old. You're too sick. You can't do this.*"

I knew I needed to change the Narragansett narrative and drown out my negative thoughts.

The night before the start of the event, I watched the film, Nyad, on Netflix. Are you noticing the preponderance of the letter N in this story?

Nyad tells the story of marathon swimmer, Diana Nyad, who in her sixties became the first person to swim the 110 miles from Cuba to Florida. Talk about the perfect movie to watch before walking sixty miles in three days.

As I labored up Narragansett Street, I decided to change the negative voice in my head to chant, "Go like Diana."

Over and over, I repeated the chant, stopping when I needed to gather myself, then proceeding up the hill until I finally reached the top. I was still nauseated but I made it.

I even got on a sweep van once I reached the top and had the medics examine me. Yep, the once fat girl who hated the thought of being swept, did the smart thing.

Of course, I had to loop the medical area several times afterwards to make up for the mile and a half I was in the van. I still needed to walk sixty miles. What can I say? I am perfectly imperfect.

That voice in my head can get pretty loud, especially when my confidence has left the dock without me. When I take potshots at myself, those surrounding me may become collateral damage.

That negative voice is like a playground bully. It keeps pounding away as long as it can get away with it. So, I call upon my best friend to help – the one that believes in me – myself. The 3-Day event has shown me how to be a better person. I have to believe I can.

Talking to Others

At one of the pit stops during one of my many 3-Day Walks, I stood behind a walker filling her water bottle. My teammates were waiting for me to fill mine so we could continue with the Walk.

The walker appeared to finish filling her water bottle and she placed it on top of the cooler. She stood there for several minutes, adjusting something on her fanny pack.

Knowing my teammates were waiting, I asked, "Excuse me. Would you mind if I slip in there to fill my water bottle?"

The walker angrily turned and said, "Sure go ahead because what you're doing is so much more important than what I need."

It was then that I noticed she had a second water bottle in her hand, apparently intending on filling that one as well.

My initial reflex was to bark back. Reigning in that snarky Satan perched on my shoulder, I responded, "I'm sorry. I didn't realize you had another bottle to fill. Go ahead."

"Well nice of you to give me permission," she snapped.

Geez, give me a break.

The Shoulder Satan was sounding increasingly convincing. I am not sure I would have been able to strangle him in my Fat Years.

Instead, I replied, "I'm sorry I barged in when you were not finished filling your water bottles. I guess my boomer eyes failed me again. Please finish what you need to do. I'm in no hurry."

"After all, the 3-Day is a Walk, not a race," I laughed, "Thank God."

The walker thanked me and said she was really feeling her aching muscles. She wasn't sure she could finish.

I understood how devastating it feels when you think you may not be able to finish the Walk. It goes way beyond the mechanics of walking sixty miles. It's honoring the loved one who inspired you to try. It's also proving to yourself you can do far more than you believed possible. Finishing is everything to you.

I asked this hurting walker why she was walking.

"My mom died from breast cancer last year."

"I am so sorry," I replied, "She would be very proud of you."

With tears in both of our eyes we hugged and said, "See you at the finish!"

Take that, Shoulder Satan. If I reacted angrily, which I REALLY wanted to do, I would never know this walker lost her mom to this horrid disease.

Stereotypes and snap judgments fail to see the individual. We do not know if they are hurting, or sad, or struggling with demons only they can see.

Whenever I talk to the individual, my view of that person changes in some way. Everyone has a story to share. All I need to do is ask.

Walking the Walk

About midway through my corporate career, I worked with someone who had a saying that made me chuckle every time.

She would roll over to my desk and say, "Now, you realize I am perfect, but..." I knew I was in for some juicy gossip.

After two-plus decades of walking, you realize I am perfect. My biases are gone. I am strong. I am a leader on the path to perfection for all.

I forgot to share another dominant trait of mine – sarcasm. Should I ever achieve perfection, you can bury me six feet deep.

If I were perfect, would I allow my negative voice to take over my narrative? Would I nag a limping walker with determination to conquer that hill to give up and get on a sweep van? Or would I have to give up the Walk because perfection made it unnecessary?

Instead, I try to walk the walk. I remember the stories and the lessons they taught. And I remember to get up when I fall, then try again.

Getting up reminds me that what I am doing matters. What I have put this Old Lady body through personifies what this event means to me. Heck, even a head-first fall down an escalator in 2023 on my way back to the airport did not stop me. Maybe it's not commitment as much as hitting that hard head of mine one too many times.

Yet all the abuse I've endured is nothing compared to a head-on collision with cancer that courageous individuals undergo.

My teammate, Penny, once expressed she was delighted, yet puzzled by walkers who have never known this disease but still come back – year after year. I remembered her insightful response she shared in an interview for my personal blog.

I asked Penny what life lessons she had learned from being a survivor. She said the biggest lesson for her (and her family) is that no matter how challenging or frustrating a problem seems:

> **"It ain't cancer."**

Exactly. That truth is why I need to connect with the remarkable individuals in our Pink Bubble. They put my problems in perspective. They reassure me that no matter what, I can survive. They urge me to walk sixty miles in three days in their shoes.

On each Walk, I wear the names I have accumulated over the years of people diagnosed with cancer, those we have lost, and the names of the inspiring survivors. I created a shirt (and a pink cape) to wear on the Walk that says it all – *Walking for the Real Heroes.*

Lesson #3 Learned: I will stumble, but I will get up and take another step.

CONCLUSION: Still Walking

When I took that first step in 2003, little did I know what this event would mean to me. What started as a planned, one-time experience to support my sister became my lifeline to a better me.

Prior to walking in the 3-Day Walks, I was merely existing, numb to the world around me, and even more numb to myself. Many days I would let out a deep sigh as I opened the door to my latest corporate job, desperately trying to get through another day. But it wasn't the job. It was me.

I wanted more but the fog that engulfed my life was trapped in a valley of my own making. I needed to climb out to rediscover a purpose that would challenge me and open me to the feelings I ignored far too long.

Freelancing as a writer was the jolt I needed, pushing me outside my comfort zone. It was so beyond the self-protected world I built when working for others. Yet, even then, I played it safe, writing for the industry I spent decades in.

The 3-Day Walk burst through the door I kept locked. It refused to let me retreat into my sheltered, little world. I developed relationships with my teammates and the Pink Bubble community that are both raw and rewarding.

You cannot hide from a cancer diagnosis. My involvement in this event has taught me I cannot bury what I feel and ignore the reasons I act the way I do – not if I want to live my best life.

The 3-Day Walk grounds me during the stormy times of life. After two-plus decades of participating, I cannot walk another sixty miles without listening to more stories, appreciating the uniqueness of every person I meet, while discovering how I can be a better me.

I am still walking – for myself and the countless others who are in pain, who are trying like I am, and who want to be a better person.

Walk on.

NOTES

INTRODUCTION

1. "About the 3-Day," Susan G. Komen 3-Day, accessed August 25, 2025, https://www.the3day.org/site/SPageServer?pagename=about

Chapter 1

1. "Our Mission and History," Susan G. Komen, accessed August 25, 2025, https://www.komen.org/about-komen/our-mission/

2. "Health Insurance Portability and Accountability Act of 1996 (HIPAA)," U.S. Centers for Disease Control and Prevention (CDC), accessed August 25, 2025, https://www.cdc.gov/phlp/php/resources/health-insurance-portability-and-accountability-act-of-1996-hipaa.html

Chapter 2

1. "Inventor Karl Müller III," Kybun Switzerland, U.S. site, accessed August 25, 2025, https://us.kybun.swiss/pages/about-inventor

2. Winig, L. 2012. Revised 2024. 'Social Media and the Planned Parenthood/ Susan G. Komen for the Cure Controversy.' 1975.0. Cambridge: Harvard Kennedy School.

Part Two

1. "Eleanor Hodgman Porter: American Novelist," Britannica, accessed August 25, 2025, https://www.britannica.com/biography/Eleanor-Hodgman-Porter

2. "Pollyanna Principle: The Psychology of Positivity Bias," Positive Psychology, accessed August 25, 2025, https://positivepsychology.com/pollyanna-principle/

Chapter 3

1. Francesca Gillett and Matt Murphy, "Olivia Newton-John: Tributes as Grease Star and Singer Dies Aged 73," *BBC*, August 9, 2022, https://www.bbc.com/news/entertainment-arts-62472100.

2. "The Great Recession: December 2007-June 2009," Federal Reserve History, accessed August 26, 2025, https://www.federalreservehistory.org/essays/great-recession-of-200709

Chapter 4

1. Alicia Nortje, Ph.D., "What Is Cognitive Bias? 7 Examples & Resources (Incl. Codex)," *Positive Psychology*, August 5, 2020, https://positivepsychology.com/cognitive-biases/.

2. "Why It's Hard to Let Go of Stereotypes," Psychology Today, accessed April 17, 2025, https://www.psychologytoday.com/us/blog/what-are-the-chances/202502/why-its-hard-to-let-go-of-stereotypes.

3. "About Us," Del Mar Fairgrounds, accessed August 26, 2025, https://www.delmarfairgrounds.com/p/about.

4. "Torrey Pines State Natural Reserve," California State Parks, accessed August 26, 2025, https://www.parks.ca.gov/?page_id=657.

5. "Types of Bias," CPD Online College, accessed July 23, 2025, https://cpdonline.co.uk/knowledge-base/safeguarding/types-of-bias/#anchoring-bias.

6. Kendra Cherry, MSEd, "Bandwagon Effect as a Cognitive Bias : Examples of How and Why We Follow Trends," accessed May 1, 2025, https://www.verywellmind.com/what-is-the-bandwagon-effect-2795895.

7. "How to Identify Bias: 14 Types of Bias," Master Class, accessed April 9, 2025, https://www.masterclass.com/articles/how-to-identify-bias.

8. Jennifer Edgoose, MD, MPH, et al., "How to Identify, Understand, and Unlearn Implicit Bias in Patient Care," *FPM*, 2019;26(4):29-33 https://www.aafp.org/pubs/fpm/issues/2019/0700/p29.html

9. "Breast Cancer in Teenagers: What You Need to Know About Risk, Signs, and Prevention," Gregory Rhodes, MD Cancer Center, accessed April 27, 2025, https://www.basscancercenter.com/cancer-blog/breast-cancer-occurrence-in-teenagers-what-you-need-to-know.

10. "Empowering Young Adults Through Research and Community: The ShareForCures® Alliance and Young Survival Coalition," Susan G. Komen blog, accessed April 27, 2025, https://www.komen.org/blog/shareforcures-young-survival-coalition/.

11. "Stories: Bill Griffith," Male Breast Cancer Global Alliance, accessed April 23, 2025, https://mbcglobalalliance.org/stories/bill-griffith/.

12. "Self-Serving Bias in Psychology," Simply Psychology, accessed April 26, 2025, https://www.simplypsychology.org/self-serving-bias.html.

13. "Projection," Psychology Today, accessed May 7, 2025, https://www.psychologytoday.com/us/basics/projection.

14. "In-group Bias," Dictionary of American Psychological Association, accessed May 1, 2025, https://dictionary.apa.org/ingroup-bias.

15. "Jim Valvono's Iconic ESPYS Speech," V Foundation, accessed May 2, 2025, https://www.v.org/story/jim-valvanos-iconic-espys-speech/.

16. "The Science of Bias," Smithsonian Institute, accessed May 26, 2025, https://biasinsideus.si.edu/online-exhibition/the-science-of-bias.

17. "About LEGOLAND Parks," LEGOLAND, accessed May 30, 2025, https://www.legoland.com/about-legoland-resorts/.

18. "Taoist Yin Yang symbol," The Center of Traditional Taoist Studies, https://tao.org/tao/yin-yang-symbol/.

Chapter 6

1. "What Makes You Unique? A conversation with David Linden about his new book on human individuality," Psychology Today, Accessed June 5, 2025, https://www.psychologytoday.com/us/blog/brainstorm/202009/what-makes-you-unique.

2. "BRCA Gene Changes: Cancer Risk and Genetic Testing," National Cancer Institute, accessed June 11, 2025, https://www.cancer.gov/about-cancer/causes-prevention/genetics/brca-fact-sheet.

3. Molly Winding, "This breast cancer survivor learned to feel beautiful again by stripping down on national TV," *AOL.com*, June 8, 2016,

www.aol.com/article/2016/06/08/this-breast-cancer-survivor-learned-to-feel-beautiful-again-by-s/21391750/.

4. "About Us," Pink Wings, accessed June 11, 2025, https://www.pinkwings.com/about.htm.

Chapter 7

1. Julia Cox, Diana Nyad, "Nyad." IMDb, 2023, 2 hr, 1 min, https://www.imdb.com/title/tt5302918/

2. Cathy Miller, "It Ain't Cancer," *Old Lady Biz*, July 3, 2014, https://oldladybiz.com/aint-cancer/

ABOUT THE AUTHOR

CATHY MILLER SPENT OVER thirty years as a professional business writer in both the corporate setting and as a small business owner. Her love of storytelling blossomed into her debut memoir that recounts her two-plus decades of participation in the sixty-mile, 3-Day Walk for the Cure. Cathy also writes at her blog, OldLadyBiz, where she celebrates the joys of reading, writing, and walking (lots of walking).

When she is not writing, Cathy cares for her amazing mother, who has passed the century mark, and their adorable Miniature Schnauzer, Penny. Cathy also creates designs for the Old Lady Biz Store, featuring fun collections for book lovers, writers, walking warriors, and anyone who enjoys a touch of old lady humor (www.OldLadyBizStore.com).

Author Website: www.CathyMiller.biz

ACKNOWLEDGMENTS

I COULD NEVER HAVE completed this book without the help of so many big-hearted individuals. Thank you to every Pink Bubble member who shared their stories, their support, and their strength to help keep this Old Lady Walking sixty miles in three days. You are the heart and soul of this book.

A personal thank you to my family and friends and those who contribute to my fundraising. Your generosity ensures this Old Lady has no excuse not to walk another 3-Day Walk. You make me believe I still can.

Finally, thank you to the equally giving writing community. You helped a terrified person who just wanted to write to find the courage and the tools to succeed. I especially want to recognize Devon, Lori, and Paula, who are my anchor of support. You always have my back and your professional feedback on my first draft offered invaluable ideas for making this a better book.

Special thanks to my "twin," Sharon, who is always there to help with her incredible breadth of knowledge, and who has shown me what it truly means to be a better person.